Talking Me Off the Roof

Talking Me Off the Roof

Poems by

Laurie Kuntz

© 2022 Laurie Kuntz. All rights reserved.
This material may not be reproduced in any form, published,
reprinted, recorded, performed, broadcast,
rewritten or redistributed without
the explicit permission of Laurie Kuntz.
All such actions are strictly prohibited by law.

Cover design by Shay Culligan
Cover art by Colombian artist Angie Rengifo
Author photos by Laura Angel

ISBN: 978-1-63980-216-6

Kelsay Books
502 South 1040 East, A-119
American Fork, Utah 84003
Kelsaybooks.com

For Steven and Noah:
On level ground

Acknowledgments

The poet is grateful to the following magazines for publishing the following poems:

50 Word Stories: "Lessons in Electricity, To Do in Quarantine"

Best of the Net Nomination 2019: "Self Portrait"

Comstock Review: "The Purpose of a Rose"

Crowsfeet: "Finding Polaris"

The Dillydon Review: "Thinking of Dead Poets Among the Homeless"

Literary North: "Asunción"

LKMNDS Podcast: "Darnella's Duty"

Lothlorien Poetry Review: "Ovation"

Moonstone Review Anthology on Hope 2022: "The Person Right Next To You"

Moonstone Review Anthology on Ukraine 2022: "Aftershocks"

Moonstone Review Anthology on War 2021: "Those We Buried, Those We Sent Home"

Muddy River Poetry Review: "Every Possum in the Neighborhood," "Miracle Muffin"

The New Voices News: "Darnella's Duty"

One Art: "That's What You Say"

Poetry Breakfast: "Self Portrait"

Rise Up Review: "Why I Don't Write About Florida's *Don't Say Gay* Bill"

Roanoke Review: 50 Year Anthology: "Infinite Tenderness"

Snapdragon: A Journal of Art and Healing: "Metastasis"

The title of this book is after a line in the song "If We Were Vampires" by Jason Isbell

Contents

Ovation	13
I Am Having an Affair With the World	14
Miracle Muffin	15
The Person Right Next to You	16
Cilantro	17
That's What You Say	18
To Do: When in Quarantine	20
Every Possum in the Neighborhood	21
If We Want to Dwell in the Grace of Love,	
We Must Tempt It to Leave	22
Asunción	23
Infinite Tenderness	25
"The Way You Talk Me off the Roof"	27
Husband Rebuilding the Engine	28
Goodbye/Hello	29
The Truth at 42nd Street	30
Without	31
On Bread and Birthdays	32
For Better or Worse	33
Anniversary	34
Anniversary, Again	35
Where to Put the Crayons	36
Milk Teeth	37
The Trouble With Happiness	38
Grappling With Gratitude	40
Darnella's Duty	41
Those We Buried, Those We Sent Home	42
Sons Have Sleepovers While Putin Deploys	
Troops	43
Consider the Pepper	44
Finding Polaris	45
Father and Son with Shovel	46
Metastasis	47

The Jump	48
Gravy	49
Amazing and Annoying	50
Style	51
After the Assault	52
Cinderella in Sneakers	53
Self Portrait	54
The Weight of Absence	55
Why I Don't Write About Florida's *Don't Say Gay* Bill	56
Recital	57
A Close and Constant Rage	58
Purpose of a Rose	59
Directions to Come Ashore	60

Ovation

If this is my last poem,
may my words continue.

I'll relax in breaths of finality—

I've joined in the laughter,
the clapping after music,
a hearty dinner, frivolities
in all its forms.

I stand in ovation
for strong backs, working hips,
and hops to places that I wish
never to leave.

I will stay—

with those who love a porch,
a bloom of bougainvillea,
a dry, but crooked path after rain,
and the presence of every two,
four, or eight-footed living thing.

If this is my last poem,
I will rejoice in the fluency of thought,
but still mourn because there is room for that
in a world that goes on with or without me.

I Am Having an Affair With the World

but now I know all illicit love ends
badly and in anger despite the beauty
seen in the coleus grown from a cutting
no bigger than my thumb,
or in the red and yellows of a sunset spilling
its leftover hues into the sea's horizon,
a backdrop to the alley cat's call colliding with night.
I know these short-term loves will end,
and I will be picking up the debris
of petals and paws and feathers left
by the sparrow who perched on my sill
for a moment, leaving me enamored
by its striped breasted fluff,
but when I was about to reach
it trilled, then flew away.

Miracle Muffin

Muffin was a rescue,
but aren't we all rescues in one way or another?

If we speak of dog years, she had many, and her name
was not our choice, but who can ever choose a calling?

Part Shiba Inu, and parts unknown, she was a promised dog,
my son's first friend, when we moved to places unknown—

strange house, unpaved streets, rural routes.
A companion he needed until he didn't.

Then, like a giving tree, she started to slow, her limbs drooped,
her gait wobbled, and her kidneys faltered, then came back filtered
like a prayer,

giving her a tad of time to fetch her bargain of days,
and each time this happened, the vet called her a miracle,

but aren't we all miracles at one time or another?

The Person Right Next to You

"There's a fifth direction: not the sky or the ground, but the person right next to you."
—Eduardo C. Corral

The person right next to you
is perhaps the direction home
or your North Star when night falls hard.
The person you sit with, not in total silence,
but at slow intervals, speaks a truth,
between sips of warm chamomile on a December-like day;
both of you watch, from a grateful window,
passersby grabbing time, moving toward that fifth direction,
hoping remaining days will not set in solitude.

Cilantro

That green clover-like plant
scents our garden and finds harbor
on your tongue.

Such a useful ingredient
to add zest, but where is the recipe
to add comfort to our shared plate?

When an acquaintance lost her husband of 45 years,
you felt a need to comfort someone we barely remember,
but see daily on a computer screen.

You posted *sending love and light,*
so unlike your technical mind or reason,
knowing how light travels and how love is rationed,

like a rare spice we garnish,
on all our acquired tastes,
much like the cilantro you plant and I pick.

That's What You Say

My mother died
in a shared room
at a nursing home,

while aides sat in the illuminated pod
their white canvas shoes resting
on the cold tile floors.

Time of death was 4:38 A.M.
Death appears in a stormy river
or on a placid lake shore.

Hours and minutes do not matter,

for death sets no alarm,
hurries no nurse to gently
palm a wrist and look for a pulse.

When we came to collect her clothes
that smelled of mold and brittle bones
and gather her meager belongings—

a half filled bottle of *ballet pink* nail polish,
one earring, a hair clip, and a velvet box,
which once held a gold charm bracelet—

I imagine her calling for one of us
to pluck the coarse grey hairs
that protruded from her chin like thorns.

Lost in reveries of tasks and memories
when my sister's tears broke,
the frail woman in the neighboring bed insisted,

She went peacefully,

but how could she know?
What possible revelation
comes to witness at 4:38 in the morning?

To Do: When in Quarantine

Composed is a list
of the important tasks,
what one should be doing these days,
but no one knows how many of these days
we have left, so why
organize the underwear drawer,
why fill the car with antifreeze?

Is it necessary to venture into the dark
dank resources and clean every closet;
can't those cobwebs above the drapes
pass for decoration?

If I am not here tomorrow
when they clean out my closets,
who is going to care
if I've color coordinated my blouses,
now hanging in empty spaces?

Maybe *To Do* in these mercurial days
means sit next to the cat, her purr, a mantra,
find that dog-eared book and continue reading,
listen to the katydids in the absence of traffic,
and certainly fill the vase with something in bloom.

Every Possum in the Neighborhood

Remember when the biggest worries
were critters that begged entry
into every garage left ajar?
Years ago, her keys and doors undone,
my sister, the youngest of us, left an open invite
for every possum in the neighborhood.

This happened before pandemic problems,
before a mandated distance between the living.
The possum, placid in its nature, hunts unwanted critters,
the snared snout just a way to self preserve
its many possum possibilities,
preservation, a trait we need in vicious and viral times.

So, leave the entryways open,
invite the useful guest in,
for we never know
just what will save us.

If We Want to Dwell in the Grace of Love, We Must Tempt It to Leave

Temptation made me dream
you had left me, and instead of freedom
that I think about in true time,
there was a smirk on the face of loneliness.

In that dream I walked back
to where we first loved,
the room empty and the air stale.

It could have been anywhere,
but it was not.
I could have been anywhere,
but I was not.

I was in a dream,
and the temptation to yell out your name
in my dark spiraling sleep
was real, and I woke.

Asunción

> "Something else is slipping away, a state flower perhaps, the address of an uncle, the capital of Paraguay."
> —Billy Collins

Details which once belonged to us
slip off memory's hanger like a silk shirt.

A famous battle,
the actor, who always plays the villain,
or is it the hero . . . that jazz refrain,
beloveds' birthdays,
names of well-navigated cities,
are lost in the tattered purse of recollection,
like the capital of Paraguay.

Not that the capital of Paraguay means much to many,
but we were there, you and I, in November,
when mangoes fell from trees lining the boulevard.

We stuffed our packs and pockets full,
then ate them under moonlight
when no one was looking,
and the world was mango-wonderful.

Now, I do forget—

forget to buy your favorite cereal,
to turn lights off, to tie the dog up—
forget that I annoy.

But, I do remember the capital of Paraguay.

We were there once, you and I,
knapsacks caboosed to our backs,
belly filled with fallen mangoes,
living for days on just that fruit.

Infinite Tenderness

For Steven

You called lost and broken down
one December night—
on a road amidst scarecrows and corn;

your car had dropped a fan belt,
and I was tasked an endeavor into darkness
to find you.

The night choked me with weather and empty country roads—
no street names, nor landmarks,
just fields, leftover snow, and taunting black ice.

A stranger brought you to safety that night
as darkness goaded me away from you.
Every winter storm since recalls your rage.

Once, in vengeance, I revealed
that Anna Karenina jumps in front of a train,
ruining the ending you were just about to read.

It was an ending you saw that night,
waiting for me to rescue you
from fan belts and wind.

Like Anna, I'm not good at saving others, or myself.
I fail at heroics—I'm better at baking a cake,
basting a turkey, or planting pansies—

if only I could steal myself
out from your anger,
rise to an occasion,

save you from a precipitous fall off a cliff
or venture to find your voice lost
in the Siberian wind.

Anna Karenina had infinite tenderness
but no one to save her,
unlike all the kindness that remains to rescue us.

The time we've had together leaves me breathless, as if running for
a train that I know will stop in places I never want to be again,
but I board it anyway and take a window seat.

"The Way You Talk Me off the Roof"

On My Husband learning the song
"If We Were Vampires" by Jason Isbell

I asked you to learn a love song with a sad chorus:

This can't go on forever
Likely one of us will have to spend some days alone . . .

and you spent all morning
tuning your guitar, refreshing the chords,
getting the rhythm down, learning the lyrics:

One day I'll be gone, or one day you'll be gone . . .

You told me, *It's too sad to sing*
about loss, about spending time alone,
about something inevitable—

so, we lightened the moment,
said the song reminded us of stories
we read to our son about a mother watching her child grow
until the child was the parent and the parent the child,
or the one about the tree that gets cut down
little by little, to gift a boy all he wants.

These days all we want is not to spend
time alone, to avoid the inevitable,
to be vampires living under many waxing moons.

Husband Rebuilding the Engine

He does things like that.
Oiled bolts spread on a tarp.
In old military issue coveralls,
not camouflaging his own disasters
of stalls and spills,
nuts and springs clamor
onto the belly of the engine.
I want him to seek a mechanic,
but he needs to conquer
this jetsam and flotsam of steel.
I come out, hold the hood up,
turn the key, push the pedal to the floor.
He listens for the hum, that perfect pitch.
He'll spend hours doing just this.
I call him for dinner,
I call him for a bath,
I call him for love.
There is no time, but this time,
watching him under a single bulb
waiting for the motor to ignite,
rebuilding all that fails him
into something that turns over and runs.

Goodbye/Hello

Right before Noah, our only child,
went off to college, on our last night at home together,
on the TV screen, an aged Neil Armstrong,
spoke about being newly divorced after 34 years of marriage.

How does that happen?

My silent response, wry as a smile,
staring at our son's eyes, hinged in the unspoken,
as he wondered if we, once he left, would do the same.

Armstrong went into the unknown,
and returned reconsidering
all that was familiar.

Dropping our son off at school is our ascent into space.

Rocketing in a dark, yet starry terrain,
the endless horizon renews
and unhinges all that astounds,
saying goodbye, we begin
the turbulent voyage of saying hello.

The Truth at 42nd Street

A reunion, friendly banter as we hurried
into the subway and separate upcoming stops
that would keep us apart for another year.

As the car zigzagged into 42nd Street
she gathered her bag and belongings
for a rush to exit.

Just before the subway car swerved to stop,
she commented on how wonderful my marriage is—
together so long, the twig and twine of history,
the role models for happiness.

Her words a lull in the engine's screech,
I started to say that all is not as it seems,
that no marriage, no history is without a battle
toward one's own terms of victory.

But, the train pulled into 42nd Street,
and she rushed off, her wing-like hug
a testimony to her belief,
while the doors slammed shut
on the truth.

Without

Found accidentally on a shelf,
this book of poems by Donald Hall,
written for his bald wife
after she had died from leukemia—
every page, a eulogy
to the details of what is never noticed
until noticing brings an ache that rips
into the marrow of memory.

Then, something simple as dust on a sill,
becomes the axis of all we live without.
Hall loved his wife, remembered
every detail of her life when her life was detail-less.

I want to tell you this, while we still share time,
but when I find you in the kitchen, you are rummaging
through the fridge, cursing me for taking a bag of Edamame
out of the freezer and letting it spoil—

leaving us without something green for dinner.

On Bread and Birthdays

All I really wanted was a slew of jonquils
or a single candle dripping waxy over
Black Forest Torte,

but you forgot my 55th.
The day passed marked by absence,
without the simplicities of heart.

It wasn't until weeks later, readying
for a trip home, your father dying,
in between packing,
the estranged years,
a day of bills and plans and tickets,
you baked me two loaves of bread,

one to eat and one to freeze,
your kneading and precise measuring
sustaining sadness and history.

On this waning Sunday,
I have just finished the first loaf
and have taken the other out,
beautifully formed and golden—
ready for defrosting.

For Better or Worse

We had no vows for our hurried lunchtime commitment,
only there at the justice of peace to make our unborn son legal.

Had we an oath, we would have never said
for better or worse,

maybe *for better or best,*
not realizing the presumptions of our shared youth.

Here we still are, the son, legal
and grown into his own vows.

While for us, the word *worse* seeps into the borders of our promises,
and *better or best* sheds its skin,

but leaves an armor as we stand guard
on a precipice and look down
at our remaining journey of steep and rocky paths.

Anniversary

I don't know a love that does not chip away
at the day to day of what couples us.
Every act of creation, also an act of destruction,
and memory is history's great reviser.

The years pass, the regrets mount,
but so does the coupled light
we both enjoy at sunset,
the sound of the brown thrasher
hidden in our magnolia tree.

We strain to catch a glimpse before it flies—
a memory implanted on its wingspread
taking with it a piece of what has been shared.

Anniversary, Again

The days pass as starlings ignore
the boundaries of the skyway.
Things we mark as love
belong in no engraved setting,
but seen in the dusting of grey hairs off the vanity,
the sweeping of the dead
palmetto bug from under the porch light,
the random sweet set on a glass table,
all marking the tart juice of our shared years.

Layers of shivers and sweets,
goosebumps and plums.
We remain together under the weight
of every season, standing some days
on a stark precipice weaving stories
into our own private landscape,
all we let in under the presence
of every necessary ripening thing—

these years, anniversary, again.

Where to Put the Crayons

that is what my son feared
                      on his first day
in the new kindergarten class,
            holding his own box of crayolas
with new color names:

burgundy, tawny flesh, crimson, teal blue,

these wonder wands twisting lines

    into anteaters or antelopes,
                    capes or crowns,

but after the mystery of the making,
                        when he was done,
where would he put his waxing hues—
                      on what reachable shelf
of his five-year-old heart
would all these colors fit?

All this magic having to be cleaned
                        up and packed away neatly,
      even though someone with a sturdier hand
                  had printed his name squarely
on the box,

a name on a box he could recognize,

                but was still not sure
                        where it belonged.

Milk Teeth

In a photo of my son, taken before
the chiseled feel of words curled his tongue,
lips press in kiss and smile
against my cheek.

Then, the morning plea of cocks
woke him as the sky cracked the jalousies
and exploded blue into his room;
he called it magic—awakening to such light.

In this colder climate, in his eighth year,
he yearns to sleep later, pulls curtains
against all brightness, against all memory
of morning, or that photo,

which chagrins him, as do my requests
of kisses and chores, no longer
imaginary piracies, but demands,
invading his wizardry of thought.

His opal eyes become a feline squint
at my inquiries of homework or hugs.
I feel his wrath loosening
like milk teeth at the nub,

for what was once magic, there are now words,
daybreak, study, errands, chores, sleep,
fixed, like the cut of teeth through gums,
giving everything a more permanent definition.

The Trouble With Happiness

In Hawaii, on a family vacation,
on one of those days
we let you eat anything you wanted,
and then drove to "Mustard's Last Stand"
serving 47 varieties of hot dogs.

On a day when

the waves were calm enough
and I wasn't worried, and let you go
further out than I ever have,
and the sun block did not sting your eyes,
and the rented car had a radio station
that played 60s songs without commercials,
and the DJ repeated the titles after each song,
and we ate French fries at three different rest stops,

knowing that this could be enough, forever—

but, for no reason, you started to cry,
then whispered, *I'm just so happy.*

At six, you knew
                      all this would become a shadowed memory
retold by three different people,

and I would argue with dad whether the hot dog stand
really had 47 varieties, and whether
the DJ played commercials between the rock and roll,

(which, too, we'd argue over),
                                every detail now askew.

You knew then,

on one of those days,

these infinite moments of our lives,
held in the pockets of your tears,

would never last.

Grappling With Gratitude

A month after her brain surgery,
Greta met us in the Sawtooths,
and we shadowed behind her scrambling
over boulders bordering the tree line.

When the wind whisked her hair away
from her downy brow, her scar was visible,
and you, her mother, keeping abreast on the trail,
grappled with altitude and gratitude for this daughter,
lean as a mountain vine, determined as sagebrush
growing on this sketchy track of mountain and world.

                                        Who to thank . . .

    Doctors, prayer givers, kind strangers in hospital corridors,

or the daughter who believed, finally, in herself?

                                 Where is the marrow of gratitude?

Does it bellow like mountain echoes,
scatter like mariposa lilies in high altitudes,

or just settle in the lines of this poem?

Darnella's Duty

> Darnella Frazier is the young woman who filmed the murder of George Floyd on May 25, 2020

How does it feel to be 17
and just want to hold your life
in your glistening palm, go to the corner
and buy a sparkling water to quench
a parched mouth that longs to sing?

How does it feel to witness
a purpose too cruel
for all your 17 rotations
around a sun you only want to bask in?

How does it feel to beg a name,
witness a life breaking,
while your opened eyes,
see loss and corruption corralled
to the borderless sky?

And, how does the humid wind feel
as you watch it carry one man's life
to a crevice where only the wind can go?

Those We Buried, Those We Sent Home

They flash the dead on the screen,
faces shining like an autumn harvest,
their serious smiles, framed against stars, against stripes.

The parades this week are cast
with those who returned, they step to the podium,
this bruised harvest, their gait gingered.

One's eye sockets are melted shut,
like the waxy remains of a holiday candle.

He hoarsely speaks of *serving with pride,*
but his words are slurred, as are parts of his memory.

The next boy speaks too loudly, says he has no regrets.
He accepts the injuries, *a totem of honor,*
his left ear blown off by grenades.

He folds and refolds the yellow lined paper,
notes to himself on what must be said.

When his speech ends, he sees the clapping,
but cannot hear the applause,
or the few in the audience beginning to gasp.

Sons Have Sleepovers While Putin Deploys Troops

Four 15-year-olds crowd into someone's house.
Sleeping bags, iPhones, and joysticks in hand,
and a smuggled favorite pillow.

They crumb all over the living room,
                    wrestle and fart.
    A Persian rug shows haunts

of past slumbers,
and the family dog, perhaps a Shepherd,
sniffing unfamiliar smells

of other people's rowdy sons,
            crouches, ears down,
and tail tucked under all fours.

Sons banish mothers to other rooms.
The party is a success,
bodies slam

            down

waging wars
on animated screens.

The boys cajole the dog,
        (under the table and whimpering)
with *Milk Bones,*

assure him it's all make believe,

coaxing, C*ome on out,*
sit by our feet; wag your faithful tail—
protect us.

Consider the Pepper

On a Friday afternoon in southern Jerusalem,
17-year-old Rachel Levy was entering a Supersol market
to buy a pepper for the Sabbath meal.
Another girl, 18-year-old Ayat al- Akhras, a Palestinian suicide bomber,
also walked into the market alongside Rachel Levy.

The soil is tilled

pepper plants
gingerly
grow

in a measured
line of ground
side by side, yet

apart
under desert
sun and rain

its bellied shape
ripens
to fireball red

a plump season of sweetness and spice
the weighty stalk peppered
in greens and red leans to ground

the pepper easily
                falls,

over soiled lands
into toiled
hands

consider the pepper
consider the possibilities

the soil is tilled,
                the soil is stilled.

Finding Polaris

You can always pinpoint it,
looking for the triangular shine.
I want to learn to find that light
on the nights I'll be alone.
For, so much depends upon
what we leave each other.
Somewhere in the story
is our true north,
directions to travel alone,
to remember to lift our faces,
gaze upward.
We need now to create
new ways to look at old stars,
even though I would rather dwell
in our past heavens when desire
was in a turn of phrase
and the indigo sky was clearly plentiful.
On those nights, you'd take my hand,
trace beginnings and endings
of constellations that lit our lives.

Father and Son with Shovel

It's the way they hold their shovels
that separates them.

The son twirls his like a fire-studded spear,
                      thrusting the blade deep into slushy banks.

The father has a tight grip around a splintered handle,
        a cane or crutch to lead him
into the deeper parts of the road, all to be dug out.

The son hollows a lane, jumps head first
      rolls into a snow angel and back floats on mounds of powder.

Offering his tongue into the cinder sky,
        the son waits for the six pointed crystals to melt
and quench a thirst he has no words for.

The father wants to shovel till blade hits dirt,
                so his path does not freeze overnight,
he measures how wide he needs to clear the way
                            for an entrance or exit.

While they both sleep—
                one dreams of a snow day,

and the other dreads the crawl through morning traffic,
                      and the time it will take to arrive

        at a place beyond the icy highway.

Metastasis

Many find the lump while doing the mundane,
raking leaves, wiping a pendant of sweat
off one's chest.

Nearby, children jump in pillowed piles of autumn hues,
and the family dog sniffs the newly combed ground.

A quotidian life twists towards a new season,
while decayed cells turn the color of burnished oak leaves.

How could anyone bemoan the tedious—
hanging clothes in an autumn sun
or beating rugs of lint and hair,
the daily chores done with ease are a miracle.

In any yard, on any fall day, rake in hand
and an ocean wind from the east
one imagines a mother, a friend, a sister
sitting in waiting rooms—

their bald bodies a shiver in sterile offices
as they all play a round of Russian roulette.

Like rationed light in mid-November,
lives wane on the frigid edge of an emptied barrel,
or the pitch of a doctor's smile relaxing every frightened cell,
allowing all to walk out of the arcade of radiology
thinking of shopping lists, errands and pick-up points,
grateful for the metastasis of each daily burden.

The Jump

When my son coaxed me to jump
from high off the ocean pier,
I fell into the salty cocoon of sea rush.

When I sliced the surface,
he yelled, "There's a poem in this,"
which has me thinking of all the jumps
I still need to make—

all the poems, I still need to write

on days such as today—rare days
when summer air squeezes through the eye
of a late August afternoon, and I find myself
among a strangle of orange nasturtium

ebbing in a waning garden, and Sage,
named for his colored coat pokes
his beige, spun-to-grey snout
into the breeze, and I am spinning

in a world of steel blue heavens,
and radiant petunias coupled in summer hues.

There's just too much color in this turning.

It's time—not jumping, but lunging,
once again, into the deep blue crystal.

Gravy

We argued whether the red dirt path
lined with a feast of bougainvillea
was private property.

We'd been traveling this island road
since you were five, but only now a posted sign
afforded a new route.

You pointed to the hand painted arrow
swearing itself to private access,
which I thought public.

It's time now for you to be right
and read the signs posted along the platter
of your life, like the magic

of finding a rusted jeweled butterfly pin
on an uneven shoreline,
while following the logic of the North star.

Amazing and Annoying

When you swatted the mayfly
away from the dim bulb,
which shed light on something you were reading,
Noah admonished you until we all marveled

at a single red ant dragging on its back
the crushed winged insect,
which you rationalized would only have lived
a span of a day.

The amazing often annoys:

and, what we stand in awe of
is found in the breadth of the mayfly's lifetime,
the wonder of the ant's labor,
or the power of the swatting hand.

Style

Your father and I admonished you
for walking ahead on the craggy mountain ridge.

You defended your eager steps,
saying you were musing
on the musical style of the *Gin Blossoms,*
and forgot that we, your parents,
were stymied by rugged hills and curves,
in a slippery moment, chide turned to philosophy.

On top of a mountain, you professed to one thing:

Everyone's style becomes familiar,
the *blooming seasons* of my poetry,
a worn pedestrian sole.

After 20 years of weaving your life
into draping wisteria and waning moons,
you now want to see the butterfly—

mortar, pestle, sulfur,
                            vinegar and brine
                                            ground to chrysalis.

After the Assault

I heard the sirens in the distance
coming closer, and I knew
who they were keening for.

Before the call,
the knock on the door,
the wail closing in,

I captured the bird song,
the sky's teal cover,
the buzz of midday flies,

the neighbor's cat scratched
on the screen door,
the air rife with motion.

I knew nothing
would ever feel the same,
as my bruised body lit before me.

Cinderella in Sneakers

She had nothing
but work and soot,
ashes, cinders, and harsh crones,
who spun envy into a cloak of abuse.

She had her night,
as if one night could suffice.

When Prince Charming sought
to fit her life into a slender glass slipper,
caped in her new found strength,
she remembered all eyes on her,
and the dance she could shimmy to.

Now, with no curfew,
she flung broom and dust pail
to her spinster-to-be step-sisters.

Spurning the glass slipper,
that one day will shatter
and settle in dusty corners,
she put on her sneakers,
stretched her strong legs
and began to run.

Self Portrait

That's me, the stick figure caught
in a cobweb.

My sparrow limbs can easily slide
out through the fragile filament,

but my fingers, stuck on sticky strands,
refuse to unclench,

and create this intricate tangle
of crisscross gossamer.

I am both,
the spindled figure caught,

and the weaver who spins a lacey spider silk,
unable to escape, and yet, comfortable

in a lattice of trapping designs.

The Weight of Absence

February snow cascades off the roof sounding
like April's thunder, and everything that reminds me
of spring is covered in a pearl wreath,
blossoming atop the tendrils of the dormant forsythia.

These winter Sundays bring an unbearable weight.

Where you are it is bone cold and rainy,
yet, the flower market still opens at sunrise
offering a litany of daffodils,
which you buy for the altars in your garden,
and find, in sodden stalls, bushels
of plump black dotted peonies
to arrange in a dragon blue vase.

Hanoi's bouquets brighten your rooms,
rain splatters against sills.
Sunday's heavy weight is blinding,
like a full bloom of cut flowers,
an array of rose hues and lavender,
colors to cloud the cold task
of being without.

Why I Don't Write About Florida's
Don't Say Gay Bill

After Toi Derricotte

Because it is more stifling than the daily temperature.
Because rhymes are meant for poetry not repression.
Because the phrase, like sour milk, puckers my tongue.
Because the correct pronoun hardly matters
when it silences everyone.
Because there are no words, and I would rather watch
the snowy egret land on my manicured lawn
and sensing danger fly away.

Recital

They are practicing
in studios, poster-walled bedrooms,
on sunlit terraces, our children,
learn to paste a smile
on their scrubbed and fresh faces
for an audience of grown ups
who marvel at the lithe and spirited bodies.

On the gilded stage of their lives,
children all over the world
should be practicing their Epaulè,
but some are taking other positions
in cellars and dank crawl spaces.

They should be gliding
across polished floors,
but today they pirouette
into evacuation routes, keeping beat
with the not so distant thunder.

A Close and Constant Rage

So there are others
like myself, in constant conflict,

but comes a day, on a walk perhaps,
the lone egret flies from a bush

and the milkweed someone planted
is laden with monarchs,

the ones not yet extinct
alarm my continuous rage colliding

with the natural world, and those left,
who attach bumper stickers to electric cars,

wear cotton and conserve water,
carry reused paper bags,

surround me with a can-do moment of hope.

They are like those kind birds with feathers
bursting in day breaking hues,

who still fly in my field of vision
making the general state of the world

appear askewly in focus.

Purpose of a Rose

After an axiom by Thich Nhat Hanh

Perhaps the killer on the run,
a ruling despot, or the warden of all sins
will never fathom the rose's purpose
in its crinoline of perfumed petals,
but the rest of us are aware of its intentions
more than the rose is of its own coming demise.
The resolve of the rose is that of the snail,
the osprey, the wind, a snaked river
or the slug of our collective reasons
to take a whiff of the momentary bloom
of a red so wild it lends us a purpose to forge on.

Directions to Come Ashore

> after a line in a poem *You Tell Us What to Do* by Faiz Ahmed Faiz

These are not times to be stranded in seawaters;
although, each day we board that boat with no life jacket.

In the distance on tawny banks
the pelicans and gulls announce their presence

remind us to stop comparing these days of solitude
to a lover who has left us with nests of memories.

In these times, we need the ordinary,
the quotidian moments

lifting a cup of chamomile to chilled lips,
listening to the peck, peck of a sparrow on the flowering plumeria

hum the ear-wormed tune till it becomes a mantra—
its melody a map directing us to come ashore.

About the Author

Laurie Kuntz is an award-winning poet and film producer. She taught creative writing and poetry in Japan, Thailand, and the Philippines. Many of her poetic themes are a result of her working with Southeast Asian refugees for over a decade after the Vietnam War years.

She has published two poetry collections, *The Moon Over My Mother's House* (Finishing Line Press) and *Somewhere in the Telling* (Mellen Press); and two chapbooks, *Simple Gestures* (Texas Review Press) and *Women at the Onsen* (Blue Light Press); as well as an ESL reader, *The New Arrival, Books 1 & 2* (Prentice Hall Publishers). Moment Poetry Press has published a broadside of her poem "The Moon Over My Mother's House" on their website: https://www.momentpoetry.com/. Her poems "Darnella's Duty" and "Not Drowning But Waving" have been produced in a podcast from LKMNDS, and her poem, "Darnella's Duty" is published in a new Black Lives Matter Anthology from CivicLeicester. Her two ESL books have been featured on the podcast ESL for Equality at https://eslforequality.com/podcast/.

Her poetry has been nominated for a Pushcart Prize, Best of the Net, and her chapbook *Simple Gestures* won the Texas Review Poetry Chapbook Contest. She was editor-in-chief of *Blue Muse Magazine* and a guest editor of *Hunger Mountain Magazine*. She has produced documentaries on the repeal of the Don't Ask, Don't Tell Law, and she is an associate producer for a documentary on the Colombian peace process and reintegration of guerrilla soldiers in Colombia. She is the executive producer of an Emmy winning short narrative film, *Posthumous*. Recently retired, she lives in an endless summer state of mind.

Visit her at: https://lauriekuntz.myportfolio.com/home-1

www.ingramcontent.com/pod-product-compliance
Lightning Source LLC
Chambersburg PA
CBHW030814090426
42737CB00010B/1264